FLOYD MAYWEATHER: A BIOGRAPHY

Let's Compare Boxing Vs. MMA

The sport of professional boxing re□uires life support for sustainability. Who cares, seriously? I mean, how many people do YOU know currently keeping up with boxer's statistics? Hard to find.

Whatever happened to inviting buddies while attending a good brawl? The truth is, today's media developed and projected a more profitable contact sport. With today's top paid boxers profiting so well from their contractual earnings, the sport still limps along. And limp along badly does it ever. Boxing's pay-per-view numbers and statistics don't lie.

When I asked several boxers (pro and amateur) about the current state of the sweet science, I got differing opinions. One of the pros even mentioned that boxing right now is just going through a "Dry spell" and will return to the pinnacle of brutal combatant-like sportsmanship of which it has lost vigor. Before determining why boxing fell off so should a person research exactly the sport's demographic. Corporate entities involved eventually jumped ship. The mass media marketing campaigns took a hike for a better opportunity, aka Mixed Martial Arts (MMA).

So what's that tell you? It's about the money.

Without Floyd Mayweather fighting, we may very well witness the funeral of a sport with such a flamboyant history. His remaining boxing career is the sport's sole stock in its entirety. Sure, I hear it everywhere I go because everyone already knows that when Mayweather retires as a boxer so will the professional sport.

A younger Floyd Mayweather even predicted this by saying, "MMA is for beer drinkers, (while) Boxing is for everybody."

What young Floyd meant by that speculative comment is that the corporations had latched onto a new market. Seriously, just look at everything projected on television now. The new "tough guy" is in, and this time hand speed and punches just aren't tough enough. Just observe how various MMA organizations now dominate the sports industry awhile Floyd Mayweather fights healthy and actively.

"Floyd is the bread of boxing. Everybody comes out to watch him fight. When he leaves, his current supporters will flock to MMA."

~Jonathan Percy, Professional Lightweight

Many pro fighters in boxing and MMA feel like Floyd Mayweather is the only hope left.

Why? Because no other fighter fre☐uents his militant training regimen; Mayweather Jr. today at 36 years old endures daily physical sparring sessions. Floyd's sparring make his actual fight night bouts seem like a 1/4 speed light practice warm up! So much for others such as Manny Pac☐uiao to carry on such greatness. No offense, Manny.

Here's Proof That "Money Talks."

People jokingly describe boxing soon becoming bankrupt because of MMA and Mayweather's enormous payouts. But that's just how vital this single man is to his sport.

"No athletes in any other sports hold value like Floyd Mayweather's family name does in boxing today. Not anywhere even close."

~Andre Preneur, Sports Analyst from TrickingisTricking.com

MMA is still yet a potentially experimental and ever-growing market. After all, it's only been at the forefront of brutality sports in the mainstream now since 2007. Though not as flourishing today there will always be at least a small margin of dedicated individuals who will preserve the science of boxing. Perhaps if the MMA organizations further capitalize on marketing, I would even foresee a boxing underground. For some are boxing fans and not temporary Mayweather bandwagon wannabes due to his overall professional record.

Mark my words: When Mayweather is gone, so is the fundamental elements of boxing.

Need proof?

The proof is in Mayweather's paychecks. Why would an entire corporate-owned conglomerate pay a single athlete so much money? That's simple. It is because "Pretty Boy" Floyd "Money" Mayweather is boxing's sole Savior, period. Style, charisma and hand speed never blended so well.

Rumor has it that Showtime is considering a decrease in business once Mayweather retires which is why they offered Floyd such a huge contract. Showtime's bid for Floyd was pretty sweet. It guarantees a minimum $32 million + per fight. Both parties agreed to a 6-fight deal. All fights must occur within a 36 month (3 years) period.

Hidden from the public are the stimulative agreements withstanding should Floyd retire, get knocked out or otherwise fail to meet the contract clause. Is that a smart move for Showtime? You bet.

Especially since its main competitor and rival HBO has now lost its one-man boxing franchise. Perhaps Mayweather Jr. himself said it best, "I box for money; belts just collect dust in the end."

Doubt him if you will, but the entire sports community will shatter upon this one man's departure from the sport that he so devoted his entire life. Greatness is alike. And so the idea of Floyd's lasting retirement only stirs thoughts remnant of Michael Jordan. He's secured his legacy in the boxing ring many times over for many years undoubtedly.

What Is Mayweather's Final Decision?

It seems that retirement is definitely on his mind within the next four years. Just evaluate the outrageous but actual figures of his recent contract. Never has a modern day athlete been by far the #1 highest paid without receiving any mainstream commercial endorsement and sponsorship via contractual agreement. The Mayweather Family name carries its own particularly distinctive brand of superiority and personality, altogether.

Is charisma worthy of challenging that of the OTHER "Greatest of all-time"?

Don't doubt it.

Pay-per-view records shattered... Check.

Worldwide pandemonium... Check.

All the money essentially a hard working honest young man could ever dream for... Check.

Solidifying and reshaping the dynamics of a traditionally manifested, once culturally-enriched physical art-form only to exit under-appreciated and forgotten for a lost cause.

BOXING MATCHES ON MAY DAY - FLOYD MAYWEATHER

Floyd Mayweather's Fight Night

A Floyd "Money" Mayweather fight night is eventful. This occasion hands down "May Day," as billed by promoters, to be the biggest day in all of the professional fighting sports.

How do you know if a Floyd Mayweather fight is as big as its surrounding hype? For starters, just ask your co-workers the workday following a Mayweather fight. Whenever there's news afloat of Mayweather weekends, nearly everyone's assumption is accurate. The casino lobbies in Las Vegas are packed with tourists, and there is more roaming security & depressed gamblers than one can fathom. But then, there are those who placed bets in favor of the champ.

A Mayweather fight is such a big deal to those who appreciate the science that it is the Superbowl of fighting sports. Just watch as countless people you engage act "cocky" displaying their arrogance reminiscent a younger Floyd. The Mayweather fight is what has kept the boxing sport alive in any sense. Once it goes, so will boxing's warrior identity.

Dare I even mention that those considered to have exquisite tastes for luxury along with a certain class of preferred etiⓆuette depart and follow suit. The world seems likely to follow the trend of MMA or mixed martial arts. The Mayweather fight night can't possibly carry on much longer. Of course, many will not appreciate the Mayweather fight until it is gone. Ironically, the Latin community will no doubt go above and abroad to replace certain festivities once attributed to May Day during the Cinco De Mayo Holidays.

But the real credit cannot just be solely attributed to just Floyd Mayweather, Jr. himself. "Money" May has a promotional marketing team self-sufficient towards keeping "Money" at the number one spot. The camp's passion has paid off well. "Money" May has been the spectacle since 2007 when Floyd destroyed Ricky Hatton. Ever since spectators foreign to boxing have ridden aboard the Mayweather's vessel.So as time progresses, we better make the most of the few remaining Mayweather fights or May Days.

The "Muhammad Ali" of This Era

Look, simply put Floyd Mayweather Jr. as overall the better fighter. Why do you ask? Well, the fact alone is that Mayweather exudes a style so commonly foreign unto most other fighters altogether; in that, he is most often not a wasteful punched. How else do you think he has been able all this time to have avoided fatigue? Floyd does not attack unless he is certain that he can accurately accumulate those easy points accredited by judges. See, that's the main difference regarding the Mayweather fighting routine. The golden rule is to box the competitor for the judges' acceptance, not the audience's.

Boxing has long unofficially been declared a spectator sport; however, the two men of the ring and its colliding forces therein have the option of fighting respectfully among each other. Crowds come and go. The entertainment spectacle is indeed a profitable one, and perhaps that is why Floyd Mayweather Jr. puts on such a fantastic showcase of affairs outside of the boxing ring.

Many have openly voiced their discussions towards the likes of Manny Pacquiao and his notoriously perceived archfoe Floyd Mayweather Jr. to be a fight forthcoming. The aforementioned is mostly mentioned in consideration of the two fighters' age. Surely, fight fans wanted to witness the potentially greatest bout ever conducted among two of the premier non-heavyweights of our generation. No matter the victor between these two gifted talents, people will undoubtedly argue that whoever lost probably could have won had the rivalry physically begun before such an enduring withholding. Either way, people still want this fight to happen.

FLOYD MAYWEATHER JR - BUSINESS MAN OR GREAT FIGHTER

I was watching the 30-minute promotional segment just before the pay-per-view telecast of the Mayweather-Marquez fight. A clip of the promotion shows an interview of Floyd - and he was □uoted as saying "if you are not watching a Floyd Mayweather fight, you are watching the wrong fights." It was at that moment it occurred to me that Floyd was 'wrong'!! It is more like the other way around. A revised version of Floyd's quote should read, "if you are watching a Floyd Mayweather fight, you are watching the wrong fights."

Floyd promptly went out and pitched a shutout over Mar□uez in a landslide victory. Floyd put on a great performance coming off a 21-month layoff against a very good pound for pound fighter in

Marquez. The question I had to ask myself after the fight was: Does Floyd want to be a great fighter, or is he just a businessman? The answer is simple. He is a businessman who has transformed from talented boxing prodigy who lived and breathed boxing to a money flashing, gambling, jet-setting, jive talking 'celebrity' persona. Some may say that Floyd has just evolved and has just become who he is. As a purist, I can do without it.

As an elite fighter and long time pound for pound king before his 'retirement' in 2008, Floyd Mayweather Jr. was a household name. When he retired, it was very similar to the screen going blank on the season finale of the Sopranos. We didn't know how it ended, but somehow, we knew there would eventually be a conclusion to the story.

He had beaten Oscar De La Hoya in May of 2007 and followed up with a 10 round destruction of Ricky Hatton in December of 2007. Before the Hatton fight and during training camp, he appeared as a contestant on Dancing with the Stars. This helped him cross over into the public consciousness of non-boxing fans. Since the De La

Hoya and Hatton fights did so well on pay-per-view, Floyd starting thinking he was the reason the fights drew say many pay per view buys. And why wouldn't he think that? He is the most talented and skilled fighter in the world and has never been beaten.

The reality was that just like Bernard Hopkins; his fights are based on skill, experience, defense, and playing it safe. Not a pleasing crowd style. His pay per view success was based on Oscar and Ricky's fan base - and many boxing fans that just wanted to see him lose. He walked away from the sport on top, but to most fans, an incomplete legacy. Now he is back, and hopefully, he can cement his legacy.

Don't get me wrong, as a boxing purist; I think Floyd is amazing to watch. I am not here to disparage his ability. He is the most skilled fighter in the sport of boxing, and also the smartest fighter in the ring today. The problem is, only a purist can appreciate a fighter like Floyd. The precision, the speed, the almost impregnable defense, the great stamina, and the wonderful footwork and foot speed that enables him to avoid punches. The average fan who watches an occasional fight here and there would say he is boring to watch. I would have a hard time disagreeing with them.

Why didn't he press Marȯuez and stop him? Why didn't he turn it up a notch and pour it on during the Oscar fight? Simply, why can't he be more exciting? During this big pay per view events, the world is watching.

The answer is that in the ring, he is pure talent, skill, and defense. At welterweight, he shows very little offense, but he throws very accurate and effective punches. Rarely do you see a combination thrown? His skill and talent do the talking, and nobody can talk him into doing it any other way. He simply just doesn't take risks which provide the fireworks that fans want to see.

Outside the ring, he thinks he is a star attraction. A must see a fighter who everybody is compelled to watch. He will only take fights that are the lowest risk, and the highest reward. I know boxing is a business, but if you fight just for money and to just sustain your 'Money' image, it takes away the credence and luster of your legacy.

Floyd wasn't always this way though. I first remember watching Floyd beat Genaro "Chicanito" Hernandez in the fall of 1998 for the WBC Super featherweight belt. It was clear Floyd had all the ability in the world with tremendous speed and fluidity that made him fun to watch.

At the time Floyd was just 21 years old. He had just won his first title. His father, Floyd Sr., was a professional fighter who once fought Sugar Ray Leonard in 1978. His uncles were professional fighters as well. Roger "The Black Mamba" Mayweather and Jeff Mayweather. Roger had been an elite level fighter in the 1980's, and 90's who had fought Hall of Fame fighters such as Julio Cesar Chavez and Pernell Whitaker. Jeff had been a perennial lightweight fighter who fought Oscar De La Hoya in 1993. At that time, I was convinced he had everything he needed to be an all-time great fighter. He had the Mayweather name - boxing was in his genes. His future looked bright, and I was very excited that a fighter had come along similar to my favorite fighter of all time, Sugar Ray Leonard.

Floyd made good use of his talents and took on all comers in the super lightweight division from 1998 to 2001, defending the title 8 times with impressive wins over Diego Corrales, Angel Manfredy, and Jesus Chavez. Floyd was at this best during this period. At 130 lbs, he had power and let his hands go. The effervescent fighter would overwhelm Corrales with speed and power and knocked him down five times before Corrales' corner threw in the towel after ten rounds. Corrales was the best fighter at junior lightweight to challenge the "Pretty Boy." Floyd walked through him like a hot knife through butter.

As good as Floyd Mayweather Jr. was, he didn't have much of a fan base. He was arguably the most gifted fighter on the planet since Roy Jones Jr. His skill was revered in boxing circles. Purists respected his talent and dedication to being a great fighter, but he was not a household name. He moved up to lightweight in 2002 and fought Jose Luis Castillo and won a controversial unanimous decision. Floyd would fight Castillo again in a rematch and win a comfortable unanimous decision. He showed the fans that the first fight, which many think he lost, was an aberration due to Floyd fighting with great pain in his hands. Even with these wins over the tough and formidable lightweight champ Castillo, his first two fights at lightweight, Floyd still didn't win over the fans. As a matter of fact, Floyd didn't headline a pay per view event until June of 2005, against the late Arturo Gatti, in his ninth year as a professional prize fighter.

It wasn't until the De La Hoya fight that Floyd's head began to grow. He was in the national spotlight since he was fighting the cash cow which was Oscar De La Hoya. A new series on HBO, 24/7, profiled each fighter in camp and their private lives leading up to the fight. Floyd knew he was a great fighter, but he never had the status of an Oscar De La Hoya or a Sugar Ray Leonard. This was his time to have camera time. To be in living rooms across America consistently for a month before the fight. Floyd was shown with his diamonds, jewelry, his cars, his mansion, his entourage -which included rapper 50 Cent, and his barber. It was around this time that Floyd's 'Money' image was born and he subseＱuently changed his boxing nickname from "Pretty Boy" to "Money." The fight ended up being a split decision victory for Floyd and sold 2.4 million pay per view buys. Floyd reportedly earned about $25 million for the fight. The money man had his huge payday. It's too bad the payday was formulated with his skills outside the ring and not inside the ring. The fight did not live up to the hype, and the majority of the pay per view buys were due to Oscar's fan base.

It's not too late for Floyd, however. He still can salvage his legacy. With impressive wins over Manny Pacquiao, Miguel Cotto, and Shane Mosley, he would be regarded as maybe one of the best fighters ever.

Maybe one day we can reflect on these potential fights by watching 'The Tale of Mayweather vs. Pacquiao' on HBO or 'The Tale of Mayweather vs. Cotto'. Hopefully, these fights will come to fruition. Furthermore, let's hope someone like Pac□uiao or Cotto can press Floyd into a memorable battle similar to Leonard vs. Hearns I or Chavez vs. Taylor I. Come on Floyd, forget the 'Money' persona and give us some legendary fights to remember.

FLOYD MAYWEATHER JR. BOXES LIKE MAGIC

Floyd Mayweather, Jr. has always wanted to box, and many in his family had the same career goals. His father once fought Sugar Ray Leonard. When he was young, his family was poor, and it was common to have no electricity in their home. This is in stark contrast to the life they can afford now.

Mayweather had an amateur record of 84-6 and won the Golden Gloves national championship in 1993. He won a bronze medal at the 1996 Atlanta Olympics. The team and fans, as well as Mayweather himself, felt that he won his last bout, but the team appeal failed to reverse the decision of the judges.

Floyd Mayweather had his first pro bout in 1996, and from then to the early part of 1998, he won most of his bouts by knockout or by TKO. He was on his way to the top, and many people saw that coming. He won his first title, the WBC Super Welterweight

Championship in 1998, and at the end of the year, The Ring ranked him at number 8 on the list of best boxers, pound for pound.

Mayweather continued to defend his title, and he fought Diego Corrales, winning every round. The reporters said that his speed was dazzling. He won and defended the WBC Super Featherweight title by defeating Carlos Hernandez, in what he described as one of the most difficult fights in his career.

In the lightweight class, Mayweather fought and defeated Jose Luis Castillo in his first bout in the division. Castillo simply was not fast enough to fight Mayweather and win. They fought in a rematch at a later date, and Mayweather won by unanimous decision.

Mayweather's fighting style was described as "like magic" by the trainer of the first opponent in the next weight class in which Mayweather fought. Mayweather also fought Arturo Gotti, who was at the time rated the number one contender by The Ring. Mayweather was simply too fast for Gotti and won when the fight was stopped after the sixth round. This gave Mayweather his third weight class title. He left that weight class and moved to the Welterweight division.

After he had fought Gotti, Mayweather fought a non-title fight and then beat Zab Judah to win the IBF Welterweight title. Mayweather landed a blow below the belt in round ten, and there was a melee in the ring after the blow and the call. Police had to help restore order. Mayweather did win the fight by official scoring. The decision was not overturned, but Mayweather's trainer, Roger Mayweather, was fined and suspended for a year.

Mayweather had become The Ring titleholder in the Lightweight and Welterweight classes, and eventually, he would enter the ring against Oscar De La Hoya, a fight that the world had been waiting for. De La Hoya was the WBC Light Middleweight title holder, and the fight generated the most Pay Per View buys for boxing, with 2.7 million households paying to watch.

Mayweather beat De La Hoya in a split decision to capture the WBC title. Many observers and analysts felt that Mayweather should have won by unanimous decision. Mayweather had better accuracy throughout the fight and landed more power punches. He contemplated retirement after this fight, feeling hat he had achieved his goals as a boxer. Instead, he would return to boxing, with wins against top contenders. He defeated Miguel Cotto in May of 2012, becoming one of the top money winners of all time.

MANNY PACQUIAO VERSUS FLOYD MAYWEATHER - A BATTLE FOR THE AGES

Floyd Mayweather -- "Money" to his friends -- never seems to stop belittling Manny Pac□uiao. Mayweather -- who was once considered the pound-for-pound best fighter in boxing -- lost that unofficial title to Manny. Or, I should say, Manny unceremoniously ripped it out of Floyd's hands and had never looked back.

Not content to let himself slide into obscurity, Floyd continues to call himself a "king." And he reminds anyone and everyone who will listen that he commands the most ticket sales of any fighter in modern boxing, anytime he deigns to set foot in the ring.

However, it's difficult to argue with Manny's accomplishments. After all, he forced Oscar Dela Hoya and Ricky Hatton into retirement by winning decisive victories over both of these fighters, which is something Floyd wasn't able to do when he fought them.

Floyd is certainly a special fighter. He's world-class, and he makes other world-class fighters look like chumps.

Manny, on the other hand, has a ton of decisive victories, but many of these were against obscure fighters who are known only to boxing fanatics. His opponent list isn't likely to be familiar to casual fans.

Floyd Mayweather seems content to bide his time and try to goad Manny into a fight on his (Floyd's) terms. He obviously wants that p4p title back, but Manny's not going just to hand it over.

After Manny's easy victory over Miguel Cotto -- a fighter whom some say Floyd was ducking -- it's hard to say that Manny settles for tune-up fights or second-rate opponents. When this battle between Floyd and Manny finally happens, it's going to be Floyd who needs to come out and prove that he deserves to be in the ring with

Manny, and not the other way around like most would have assumed only a few short years ago.

There is a ton of money to be made by all involved when this fight finally happens. But, more importantly, for boxing purists, this fight will settle once and for all the p4p title. If Manny wins a victory over Floyd Mayweather, especially because he is an undersized fighter who moved up in weight, it will be clear that he is not only the p4p best fighter in the world but that he deserves to join the pantheon of great boxers of all time.

FLOYD MAYWEATHER - IS HE THE GREATEST BOXER IN THE WORLD

Floyd Mayweather has always been a happy man. The reason as to why the man is always happy is the fact that he is considered as one of the greatest and the number one boxer when it comes to pound for pound boxing. He is said to be the holder unbeatable boxing records. Note that the boxer is paid much money to beat the hell out of other boxers and retain the records. Mayweather lives in Las Vegas in a big mansion that it is considered tauntingly to be a small hotel. The boxer is also known all over the world since he is known as a man who carries around a huge amount of money in his pocket.

The guy carries so much money that when you look at the pocket, it looks like a squirrel's cheek. The types of luxurious cars that the man drives are many and of different kinds and it is believed that he cannot drive the same car for one month. The bling that Mayweather walks around with and those in his closet are so many that if today he decided to open a jewelry store his jewels would be enough to start the business and they would sell at a high price since they are of the highest □uality. The star is also known for flipping the switch on his moods. There are times that you will find him very happy and even charming whereas there are other times that he is always cheerless and sullen to the point that you fear to talk to him.

Unlike the likes of great boxers like Manny Pacquiao who is never in bad terms with the authorities, Floyd has always found himself on the wrong side of the law. The troubles began in the year 2002 when he pleaded guilty to charges which were related to domestic violence. Due to this, the judge ordered that he had to undergo intense counseling at the local counseling agency. This order was followed by a sentencing that the judge ruled, where he was given a one-year suspended jail sentence for having battered some women at a nightclub in Las Vegas. He was also forced to pay compensation to the women.

For the last few years, he has not come into confrontation with the law, and this has proven that he has matured. Floyd Mayweather Jr is famous for having won his first world title at the age of 21. People had forgotten him until recently when there was the talk of the fight between him and Manny Pac□uiao who at his best form having won his bouts with knockouts and not losing any. The fight is eagerly awaited as there is intense rivalry between the two as to who is the world best boxer and the best when it comes to pounding for pound. Even so, the ring will decide who the best boxer is, thus we just have to wait for the indecision to end, and the match to be announced.

THE BATTLE BETWEEN MANNY PACQUIAO AND FLOYD MAYWEATHER JR

Known to be one of the most combative sporting activities, boxing involves the exchange of punches or jabs between two athletes with the aim of hitting the opponent. The harder one hits the opponent, the more advantage he or she gains over him/her. A battle between the world's current top-ranked boxing athletes, Manny Pac□uiao and Floyd Mayweather Jr. can prove to be the brawl of the century as awaited by many fans.

Checking on the profiles of the two boxers, it is hard to figure out who will emerge the winner when put in a ring together. There have been many feuds involving the two fighters, but there has never been a ring fight of the two. The so much awaited duel will hence create an opportunity of figuring out who the best of the best is. Manny Pac□uiao versus Floyd Mayweather Jr. will be an interesting fight to watch since each of the two claims to be better than the other. The different training techni□ues employed by the two individuals always for them in all their duels. This is because they have won a huge percentage or most of the many fights they have engaged in. For Floyd Mayweather Jr. though, he has never lost a boxing match in his career.

The undefeated run of Sinclair makes him a difficult challenge for Emmanuel. Winning every match assigned to him at one point made him the top most ranked boxer around the world. That was before he retired and gave away his championship title the World Boxing Champion (WBC). On doing so, he dropped a level lower but remained among the top two athletes in the industry. This, however, does not tarnish the chances of Manny Pac□uiao overcoming Sinclair (F.M Jr.).

Emmanuel, as he is known by many of his home fans, has one weapon with him, and that is his power punches. Although Sinclair is known to have the best tactics to defend himself, he knows that Emmanuel is a serious puncher. His cover should be ready for vigorous jabs from his opponent. On the other hand, Sinclair's speed and power are also added advantages over his opponent. He can sustain strong punches and endure till the last round. With his speed, he can maneuver and escape the jabs thrown at him hence tire up his competitor. No matter how repeatedly Emmanuel is going to knock him, he is known to have the ability to keep up with it and later come out victorious.

The two boxers are known not to be careless especially when in the ring with any opponent. This makes them dangerous towards any opponent they are fighting against in a ring. For Sinclair, he is one of those athletes able to throw punches at a higher rate while for Emmanuel repeatedly; he can counter attack anytime he sees an opening, a gap or any exposed part that will earn him a point or two against his competitor. The duel, therefore, will be one of the highly rated types.

Made in the USA
San Bernardino, CA
12 December 2017